Prosody at the cafe du coin

Also by Jeff Bien

AMERICA & OTHER POEMS

CELICO

PROSODY
*at the
cafe du coin*

by Jeff Bien

QUARRY PRESS

To my mother Ida Bien (1917–1995)
who watches over these poems still.
And to Laurie, Claudio, Meyer, Steve,
Chris and my brother, all of whom
have graced me in their love.

The publisher gratefully acknowledges
the support of The Canada Council,
Ontario Arts Council, and Department
of Canadian Heritage.

Canadian Cataloguing in Publication Data

Bien, Jeff, 1957-
     Prosody at the cafe du coin

Poems.
ISBN 1-55082-173-3

     I. Title.

PS8553.I352P76 1996   C811'.54   C96-900558-X
PR9199.3B426P76 1996

Cover photograph by Serge Clément,
reproduced by permission.
Author photograph by Kirk Fachnie
reproduced by permission.

Design by Susan Hannah.

Printed and bound in Canada by
AGMV L'imprimeur Inc.,
Cap-Saint-Ignace, Quebec.

Published by Quarry Press Inc.,
P.O. Box 1061, Kingston,
Ontario K7L 4Y5.

And angels and still more angels
gather in these tiny hours
of hierarchy and truth
and angels
who know poetry is pure sentience
and laughter, godliness.
Angels will gather.

C O N T E N T S

Acknowledgements

The title poem, *Prosody at the cafe du coin*, was selected by Ted Hughes and Seamus Heaney for special commendation in the 1988 Arvon International Poetry Competition.

Grand Manan, Where would we be without love, and *On the verge of any mental breakdown* were chosen in the National Poetry Contest (1988) sponsored by the League of Canadian Poets.

Pure Science was chosen in the TELS (Tokyo Literary Society) competition (1988) to be published subsequently in *Edge*.

Ropes was selected to be included in the poetry video project as part of the 1989 Ottawa Fall Festival of the Arts.

Fidel in a grey flannel suit was chosen in National Poetry Contest (1992) sponsored by the League of Canadian Poets.

Buttons received the Jane Jordan award, selected by Gary Geddes, as part of the National Book Festival, 1992.

Poem on St. Laurent was nominated by *Descant* for the National Magazine Award, and later translated for publication in *Rec* (Belgrade, Yugoslavia), 1995.

Marrakesh won The Citizen Award, sponsored by the Canadian Author's Association, and was selected for a Stephen Leacock Award for Poetry in 1995/96.

Other poems have appeared in *Poetry Ireland, Poetry Canada Review, Descant, Fiddlehead, Grain, Printed Matter, The Antigonish Review, Bywords, Afterthoughts, Anthos, Sivullinen* (Finland), *Ash,* and *Zymergy* as well as the following anthologies: *Garden Varieties* (Cormorant Books, 1988), *Arvon Anthology* (Arvon Foundation, 1989), *Vintage '91* (Sono Nis Press), *World's Edge Anthology* (Membrane Press, 1991), and *Remembered Earth, Volume II* (University of Ottawa, 1996).

A number of poems have been read on Radio Anthos, Q-101 FM, and CBC; others have been recorded on the audio cassette *America & other poems* (Silent Sound Studios, Montreal, 1996).

PROSODY AT THE CAFE DU COIN

On the falling of Icarus

It is a day, no more.
Ordinary in the order of its suffering.
By the sun those who must, fly.
On earth itself, small mention of miracle.

Someone acclaims the moon
and wolves appear.
A small boy asks of love
and we shrink in size.
Those who can, arrange the folly.

On such a day, thin with disguise,
was the world made.
On the advice of a serpent
was morning taken
from the rib of Eve.

In rare appearances
gods spoke, others listened.
Lumbering the planet
they obeyed. Hobbling by
the mast of their sins.

Civilizations were built,
later destroyed.
A tryst with the scullery maid.
Songs of unrequited love.
By the hand of the beast
did we become man.

Still there is the moon.
Still the sun beats heavily on our brow.
Still we search the horizon for gold.

The small gathering is a victory.
The facts are an armoured division.
The sea vaunts no man.

And though we travel the same road
we are many different conspirators.
The landmarks rise
to our various attentions.
The past leans against the wind.

By this measure
must we begin again.

And only when we look long and hard,
when the sun finally rises
will we see a boy,
a small child
falling calmly out of the sky.

Until a prayer descends

Until a prayer descends, only hearsay
a leaf amongst many trees,
a dark raven on a moonless night.

Until a prayer descends
only tired doves and slavish stars
colliding with the invisible meaning.

Until a prayer descends it is a burning angel
in a desert of names,
a last ember that is turned and turned
as it lights up the inhuman face of the sky.

Until we can hold it like a fallen bird
like a heart beating,
it is not yet a prayer.

Until a prayer descends
it is only a stone unthrown
a sea we have not yet braved,
littered with many martyrs and saints.

Until it shall become a prayer
it is only rumour
stumbling with beauty and death.

Until a prayer descends it is only
the end of the world drawing near,
an unspoken witness,
a leaf among many trees
that has yet not fallen.

Rumours

And modern man thinks his way back
to god, with impunity.
This is his talisman, his special charm.

This is his predicament,
what he knows of good luck.

The danger is we were once serious prophets
less likely to succeed.
Before we learned to speak before large crowds,
observe history from a distance.

And we are reminded
again and again,
in bay windows and large dining halls.
Reminded too, in open air theatres.

Of the ruminations of the town clerk,
the grumbling of the serpent
his sharp tongue wedged between
fantasy and serious art.

And the children at large
whisper alchemy,
turn flowers into gold,
strength into the worst kind of evil.
No care for literature, their hearts bleating
familiar rage.

We lean into the conversation
make omens out of ordinary things,
ask opinions of others.

Walking by streams, by falls
in early spring before the flood
of cicada and forsythia. We root
for the snake, pray carefully for change.

The signs are a fence.
The wind a portent.

And the tide now returns,
recovers itself
amidst the bramble of tongues
this haggle of opinion.

The sea retreats
revealing a doting wife,
a prerogative, choices
only a clockmaker might know
the difference between.

Apologia

They speak like poets, parrots on their tongues
language that will do tricks
for room and board.

They learn slowly. A new language
is always difficult.
The architecture is dreamed tediously
over time.
A landscape coerced into existence.

They will tolerate no freelanced emotion,
no popular version of the truth,
no ordinary alibi.
No experience may be proffered as evidence,
no amount of grief
to identify the dead body.

Only artifice and mythology
an apologia for the senses, a maxim
for every false beginning.
Until the world is so obfuscated
that even the slightest ambition is an indignity
to be lumped together with sex and
other four letter words
for the dullard and nihilist
to fight over.

Their vigilance must be commended.
Only their parrots can speak.
Of course it is all learned,
not a word from the heart.
Still they build their Babels, higher
and higher.
Until convinced of immortality and
not too far from god to know the difference
they jump.
Feathers and Jung, falling from the eclipsed sky.

In a City of Avalanches

I

In darkness, uncertainty begins.

Here by distant shores
in motionless detail
an archipelago of silence
crests beneath the skin,
rises to our pleasure.

The morning tarries
readies its dowry.
Steadies itself by anxious light.

The ceremony begins
begins itself,
cast by large horizon
where darkness shone.

Only later, much later
do we cast our own shadows.

II

We walk by mountain, by dark tower,
by chosen stream.
By courtyards we wander,
rally against minstrel death
the mannequin desire.

Here we wander
playing hangman with the stars.
Arranging castes of moons
of planets,
shapeless grey matter
harrowing the sky.

We wander,
summoned by love, by beauty,
circumstance whistling pale between our lips
to the tune of temptation
the bravados of war.

And arrive.
In the wilderness
where one might come upon an ending,
betray the silence,
invoke its name.

III

Let us rage then
in a large fevered voice,
accuse others of spectacle
build lighthouses for prayer
where old scholars, bandaging our feet,
might bid us Godspeed
where brave fedayeen, noble savages
might rest.

Let us rage then
to this end, no more.
Berate others for our failure to speak,
walk feverishly into the desert
disarm the silence
whisper painless incertitude
for the sake of sparing lives.

Here in the dawning of an age
where only the dead might speak
with precision
of the acoustics of an avalanche
in a city of avalanches,
where only a tongue might rise
from the pale tragedy,
the dull proceedings of law.

And though it is lost in the telling
the legend persists
lingering like fragrance, marginal,
hanging like innocents
by our unmade beds
in this archipelago of silence
where only men might rise
from the sea.

Prosody at the cafe du coin

When a poem takes place
history tips its hat to the world.
A curious revenge is heaped upon many onlookers.

Many patrons remove their clothes.
Many partisans conspire to become friends.

I came here to deal a blow to fascists
to watch the maitre d' grow old
to undermine an old regime.

I came here
to mend a conspiracy
with a silver thread of wisdom and
a secret habit of revenge.

I came here
to circulate false rumours,
about the heart, about the way we gather evidence,
about the way the facts arrange themselves
around a mood.

Instead, I am soliciting opinions
from the kitchen help, investigating
the claims of martyrs,
making war heroes out of any new arrival.

Everything is suddenly black and white
                an empty space
choreographed by many ambitious eyes.

Old newsreels of clubbed feet and twirling carrousels.
A rag-tag band of revolutionaries,
courtesans and periwigs,
clamouring to the tune of howitzers
and the Wurlitzer machine.

An impromptu gathering of newsmen and amnesiacs.
A warren of empty faces,
in the sallow shadow of dusk's wooden leg.

They are in the presence of a poem.
Of a heart that believes we are only here once.

Somehow a poem begins this way,
plans its arrival in the world.
Begging like a monk, threatening
like a terrorist,
hurling insults like any angry mob.

It is a commerce like any other,
inspired by pennies
to grow old.
Plodding, like a charity, through the news of the day.

Slandering its employer in any rent in the universe,
any cafeteria-like atmosphere,
any place to improve upon its suffering.
Dragging its feet to old promises.
A jealous inhabitant of the universe.

Everything is worth a poem.

It argues poverty, but proffers contrition.
It says it is monastic, but loses ambition
publicly.
It makes much out of tolerance
but is in constant dread of any new advocacy.
It remains non-partisan
waits patiently,
for a new tutelage, any authority
to call its own.

Once it was an explorer
today it deals in ocean-front property.

Once it spoke of freedom and immortality
Now it jealously guards its itinerary.

Once it cried complacency,
today it makes a faith out of greed.

Overnight it begins to look like a holocaust.
By morning it is a legend.

This kind of strategy is well-known in the Palermo cafe.
It pays little attention to detail.
It walks softly on clouds.
It greets you friendlily at the door.

You are the seminal figure in a turn of world history.
You enter Nero Claudius Caesar.
You somehow manage the utensils to your mouth.
You know you are the same piece of information
when you leave.

The waitress knows this is a coincidence of facts.
She knows you are a charlatan,
an accomplished liar.
She numbers her dialogues this way.
She knows her part in the casualty.

She has been an accomplice in any number of small victories.
Her dance card is not yet filled.

You return to the business at hand.
At times dressed in gold,
at times dressed in black.
Marvelling always, at how you have become a customer
in this tryst with the eternal.

A hand tucked under a waistcoat, a surfeit
of ambition.
A looking glass for the world.

The first poetry reading

And now we must read
to the gathering
to the audience on hand,
to prove we are not idle
to prove we have not died
we must read.
At any gathering
at any public site.
To our favourite aunts
to our living room chair
to the diminishing light
we must read.
With our foreheads bare
with our shirt-tails tucked in
with our hearts between our legs,
riding shotgun
on a rickshaw
over the backs of the poor,
playing Houdini
to the rich,
shouting names
to the ones we love,
we must read.
Deciding
between courage
and our newest keepsake,
enumerating why we are not
working men, why we are not peacemakers
or mechanics
or plumbers with plain old jobs
and the bills and the churches
and the mouths to feed.
Why the words were too large,
the thoughts too grand,
the emotions too simple.

A passing glance,
a trip to the museum,
a souvenir
with matching pants.

And what you were ready to die for
is now on the tip of your tongue
doing cartwheels,
standing on its head
clapping its hands
hesitating
as its pants fall to the knees
as its heart tumbles from the mat
crawling, back inside
inside.

Ode to Style

Everything is style.
Everything is a way of doing, the manner of things.

Moses had style.
So did Jack the Ripper.

Marie Antoinette had style,
and Blanche DuBois.

The poet must know style
or he will simply be a complainer.

Hamlet was a prince of style.

Hemingway had style,
the way he said goodbye to the world.

Style is the difference between Rilke
and the undertaker.
Style is what your favourite aunt almost knows.
Style comes between brothers and lovers
and, always, old friends.

It is in the air.
It is in the way we touch.

Style is an etiquette,
a signature, a chant.

A promise can have style.
So too can betrayal.

Style is not an invention of Kings.
Style is for chambermaids and hat-check girls.
The bartender knows style.
Gypsies knew style. And Chassidic Jews.

Before the Reich.
That too was style.
Religion will not teach you style.
Anarchy is styleless.
Slaves have no style.

Style is what we look for on a dark night.
The executioner holds style in his hands.
Style is the lament of Queens,
the dream of the prodigal son.

Prometheus had style.
Style killed Goliath.

Style is not for aesthetes.
Style is a doppelgänger,
a hanger on.

Romance is style
though love is its certain death.

For women style is what makes them beautiful.
For men style is a hangover.
The ordinary man mistakes style for duress.
Style is hunger, not goodwill.

Style can be dying, but only rarely.
Gods knew style when they made the planet,
fixed the rules.
Saviours know style.
Ending a poem relies heavily on style.

There is no style to silence,
suffering and death.
Style will not make you a man.

Style is a disease of the rich.
Style is the mouth of the world.
We are all in danger of finding style.
Style is what we mean when we say we are free.

Ropes

Someone invented a noun, and there it was, the world.
Another invented a verb, and there it was, explanation.
And soon they were discussing reasons,
good and bad (deathcamps were not far off).

And rules, someone thought of rules.
Rules of war, rules of the heart,
rules to grow old by.

And opinions,
opinions on late-model cars
opinions on can openers, opinions on how to die,
truckloads of opinions.

Bankers and clerks
arguing about bosses and god.
Small men hailing taxis
with the courage to mention names.
Pugilists, ninja warriors,
old scholars with squirt guns
arguing their childhood.

And finally, someone invented ropes
for housewives and truck drivers,
(no one had to invent pain and death).

Roomfuls of ropes, a planet of ropes.
Ropes for the over-30, ropes for the clinically depressed,
ropes for the "she left me", ropes for the "I fooled you",
for the taxi driver, for the minimalist abyss,
ropes hanging from the heavens (this is called crucifixion).

More ropes than deities,
more ropes than ways of praying.
A rope for each god,
A Protestant God, a Catholic God,
a Jewish God.
And children know this can't be true.
They can count this high.

And the teacher teaches us we are entitled to our opinion.
And the theologian teaches us tolerance.
And the mother and the father hold hands and tell us how
to hang from a question mark.
And the honest heart asks why.

A thousand years and the board game will still be the same.
They'll be playing monopoly on a different planet,
a new set of rules,
more expensive real estate.

And we are prisoners with no defence
because there are no witnesses,
no law large enough against the sky
to explain this wisdom.

We are all at the end of this rope.

Parenthetic

It is language
because it is there
where you left it
in the shape of a mouth.
It is confession
because you have found it.

And what was memorized
is quickly forgotten
on a night such as this.
The facts descend upon us
like vultures, like darkness,
as yesterday falls
like confetti
on our hangover,
on the circumstance of our discontent.

Yesterday,
its glimmering jewels,
its black cocktail dress,
its shimmering crown.
Yesterday, where we ruled the world.

And the morning comes
a lean predator,
hearts are pardoned
much is made of adieu.
Ten men gather to confess,
love is betrayed,
too many die.
The learning goes on.

One grows to be a poet
evolves into a species
into a past, a lesson.
In minutes we learn to crawl
from the sea, from the flood.

And come upon a god,
a level space
to wait, to stumble,
to step barefoot.

Only to fall into pits, into hunger,
into love
to return from whence
we came.

To be returned
to the darkness, limb by limb.
While journeymen read the light
and the heart beats a merciless tomb,
until deaf with music
we place one foot in front of another
and dance, through the days,
the nights, the small eternity
by which we measure
the unlikely beginning.

Rooms

And the poem has its clever start
twists and turns,
capitulates
sheds its light all at once.

The strategy is too familiar.
An old dog barking at the moon.
An ancient religion.
Silence.
Something in the order of the first person.

Hauntingly familiar.

A fairy-tale princess,
the captive tower.
Now an obelisk, now a train of hair.

We awake in a flood of daylight,
screaming syllables.
Follow love mournfully
to a place where a nightmare
might begin.

Hand in hand, purged
less-the-hero.

Already it is nostalgia,
already the narrow road.

Surprised finally to learn
that pain is only change,
echoed
in the most distant corridors.
Rooms you only imagined existed.

Sobriety

The scene is as always
hues of blue, patient grey.

The floor stretches between two extremities
by which we measure complicity.

As night enters
a sky might appear.
An appeal for understanding.

Bugles sound.
An army assembles.
Soldiers. History.

From here we see only distance.

All battles begin this way.
Scheming. Sobriety.
The wagging of tongues.

This we knew before we began our journey.
Somehow salvation is just this simple.

Almost Spring

Some thought of pulling dandelions,
arranging their lame colour
into a crown of thorns.

Some thought of murder
but quickly decided on a symbolic literature
laden with garrets and wretched kings.
Weaving, at length, inclement weather
and shawls for ladies of the night.

Some decided to stand up as kings
with a broadsword of ambition,
to stand as purists in a field of staggering light.
To do away with the nuisance of decision
and pedestrian emotion.
And on this promise fall.

Some decided simply to plant flowers
to be rendered helpless in another season.

And amidst the sprouting and the pulling
the many days of furrowing delight
there arose a voice,
a favourite topic of conversation.

It is almost spring
and the ploughing goes well.
The seasons wait their turn
and the nightingale warbles
in a well-fasted light.

It is almost spring
and God's creatures have returned to the feast.
So too have the forests and streams
in a rapturous silence, the lamenting
of a long winter's night.

It is hard to understand poetry
when all goes this well.

The heart who kept us alive.
The feet who made haste to flee.
The lungs who screamed on our behalf.

The throat is a sore loser.
The mouth is a tattletale.
The arms drag at the feet
like faith, towards the end of the sermon.

The shadows arrange themselves this way
compelled by the order of the day.
The layman is driven to his task
ordered to sing,
to champion a cause.
Lured like common beast to water
with a lust that is no longer his own.

We come to God this way
with a name for the world.

We call it love, but it is only need.
We call it need, but it is only fear.
We say it is the heart,
but surely it is bad faith.

And the night is no one's special friend
and the stars, far away burning
like a lonely candle,
climb into eternity in spirals of light
towards a simple charity.

It is curious and almost convincing
how we persist.
Shimmying slowly up the sky
like a steadfast love, falling
again and again,
clutching at moon and stars
sprouting parachutes,
all the way down.

Buttons

The Polish aristocrat,
the poet with paper epaulets.
Arguing legitimacy like nationhood
roleplaying,
with a piece of eternity stuck in the throat.

And the heart returns to familiar territory
a massacred people, few survivors,
few old enough to remember
even fewer facts.

Too many blood feuds.
Too many emotions running for the presidency.

Tempted to misbehave
tempted to quote Heinrich Heine and call it a day.
To reach for wishbones with mittens,
to hang on to eternity with a colourless thread.

A confession dragging itself to the stand.
A strategy that will defeat itself at the poll.

An old tiny canister of too many buttons
conspired to fasten our nakedness,
spools of silver lining unravelling the universe
star by ubiquitous star.

On the verge of any mental breakdown

On the verge of any mental breakdown
there are two things that must be remembered;
sanctity and ritual.
This is the wisdom of the heart.
Even as it breaks
it murmurs an old agenda.

It reminds us of many signs, many familiar signatures,
many suits of clothes.
It lists our benefactors and advises us
of our rights,
a discussion of personal property
and how the carcass is to be dragged from the bush.

It charges us nothing and
waits for us in court.

As a child
I was taught to be afraid of the dark.
I was taught discretion, respect,
moderation in decrees.

I thought we grew old and became wise
like the stories promised.
I believed the rumours in the pews
held widely to be true,
whispered,
like any small town secret.

I thought we would be forever indebted to our grade school
teachers.
I thought we would paint the world with crayons
and bring it home to our mothers.
They would pat us on the head
and congratulate us on a good day's work.

I waited for the punch line.
I waited in earnest.
I filled out many job applications.
I read poets slowly
and held my tongue with my fist.

I waited and grew lonely.
While others became bank clerks
I fought the exaggeration of the sun.
As a child
I was taught to be afraid of the dark.
Now it has inherited me, like an old fool.

Nothing has changed.
The miracle is still whispered.
The land is still on the run.

God it hurts how beginnings are made,
how we become children
many years after the fact.
How childhood curtsies in the dark.
How everything is word of mouth.

It is impossible to say what keeps us alive
hanging from our skin,
hearts with legs,
doodles of men.

It is impossible to say what we mean,
how we shuffle paper
to make room for
the hook that holds up the sky.

You threaten to break like some favourite piece of china,
come grovelling back for any new piece of testimony,
or are locked away forever
with your tongue in your mouth.

Unless, like an old Buddhist Monk
who laughs and winks,
and in the swirl of his own reflection
rewinds the tape, backwards
until everything begins again.

Pure Science

In the pure sciences there is no quarrel between opinion.
No discord between friends.
No colloquial expression to bring down the world
like a gavel, at our feet.

You repeat everything only once.
The rest is study time,
strategy in large print
a signature to lay rest conjecture.

We have built a house old friend
with tin cups at every door.
We must beg to enter.
We must beg to leave.

It is old this therapy.
Almost as old as the world.
Though of this we cannot be certain.
For ours is not a pure science.

We must answer to our hearts.
To the pounding in our chests
that tells us we are not gods
or scientists, just men
with a past.

We are however safe in the theory
that we grow old,
the tenancy between subject and predicate.
For this we pay rent
with smiles and daggers
a lexicon of old flags.

And still it is a charity to believe in.
There is the morning coffee, lunch specials,
the occasional trip to the asylum.
Though mercy must be decided
before paying the fare.

There is the choice between dying
slowly or quickly.
There is love, hate,
and much indecision.
These are our gratuities,
what we leave behind.

It has become a full-time job to massacre the world.
To jump from the first floor.
To make peace with an ambitious hand.

It has become an occupation to remove our clothes.
An indignation to recite from the heart.
A striptease for any paying pair of eyes.

We climb down from our statues
distribute our free literature,
throw snake eyes at the world.

Somehow we are still proving.
Somehow we are lightning rods for detail.
Somehow we are still at the mercy of our own voice.

Somehow in the presence of greatness
we are returned to our small hearts.

Christ hangs over us like a silhouette
placed like a paper napkin appropriately
beside our appetite.
Faith with supervision,
permission to kneel and not be seen.

Real Estate

Real estate is a serious venture.
It promises anarchy without whips, afterlife
with an attorney.
It needs a whole economy to make room for its love.

It makes men penniless with many walls
walls of faces, walls of flesh
walls you can't climb.
The wall for which there is no suitable furniture.

It promises scenery,
and a ticket to the country.
Immortality with a view.

Empty closets and photo albums
(artillery for your old age).
Many witnesses, many free stickers
and many late nights with a cigar.
Many bricks, many broken windows
and hearts,
and many calendar days.

Stockings full of promises, promises
you can count on.

And when the promises are no longer enough
there is the higher philosophy
and the middle ground of the bedroom.
You are left with what you were promised.
The scenery with a view.

Fidel in a grey flannel suit

He has never read a poem
but smokes a cigar like a Latin revolutionary,
blowing smoke rings through the heavy silence
which accompanies his heart.

He has an arm up his sleeve
grudgingly mistakes
morality for consequence.
And when he speaks of politics
he really means
a bathing suit,
one size too small.

When he is not impressing, he is an old Nazi
covering his past with bumper stickers
and a morality once removed.
A faith reserved, like a chair
for the future, where he is already
waiting for his inheritance.

He speaks brilliantly of property
and castles
though it is an atmosphere of torture
that truly fascinates him.
He dreams of sojourns with death camps
bodies naked with earrings.
Art without reparation.

I have turned thirty, many lovers
many diseases.
And he is impressing me with this.

And all at once I understand
how the postman comes to hate the disadvantaged
how the dog gets even with history.
I understand how uniforms make an army out of the news.

I am laughing all the way to the publishers
with this tiny bit of information.
I am excited at the possibility
of growing old.
I am in the asylum already,
with what looks to be revenge.
I am reconciling old pain
on my abacus, reckoning
the smallest indignity suffered
at his hand.

Still, he is a proprietorship
the signed papers
an old piece of legislation.

I raise my heart and toast the world.

Almost the perfect ending

His marriage is an arrangement with the law,
a consensus with the almighty.
A rambling dialectic between long-stemmed roses
and a threat.

Two thousand years and the stars
come between us.
The unforgivable acts of English etiquette
the faith that needs a new empire
to blaspheme.

We embrace, an old proletariat,
mumbling change and revolution.
Something about breast size and debutantes,
the murder weapon, and how to talk dirty to a whore.

Later, we discuss scores:
name dropping in Nazi Germany,
the cheerleader voted most likely to succeed at Treblinka,
the dominatrix who hangs from the ceiling from 9 to 5.

It is long, the road, from Gethsemane
to the new world.
From the squelching poverty of Havana
to skipping rope chants in Long Sault.

You teach me
what history books cannot.
That complicity is God-given,
made in our image.
The rich and poor are both filling their pockets
on this advice.

You point out the important differences
between Robin Hood and Jesus Christ.
You remind me that English is the business
language of the world.

Some fill their plates with ideology.
Some fill their plates with the cold hard facts.
Some die hungry.

You place stones, then flowers
then silence.
The conversation is this predictable.

There is the matter of your suffering.
There is the world.
There is my stubborn reply.

This is poetry.
This is what I do for a living.

Go find the day now
and wear it like an old grin,
an artifice worth saving.

Go back to your castle,
carry her playfully over the moat
as a new generation of poets dies.

Then, hang yourself in the living room.
Slowly now,
so I don't miss a line.

After the Revolution

They were whipped over three oceans.
They were flogged to the four corners of their imagination.
Now they suffer like no particular martyr.
Now they are almost human
pinned like butterflies
to a page of history.

Soon they will have forgotten their promises,
Soon they will be men with a past.

On the beaches of Varadero
I consider this folly.
How the old mumble protest to the winds
singed by wisdom,
jealous of their own reward.

How matriarchs curse their abandon
in tin castles
dedicated to the wiles of romance
and falling stars.

How everything is greed.
How a cup of coffee can save the world.

Far away a child plays with angels.
The Jews of Cochin prepare phylacteries
to greet the dawn.
The Bronx wails, struts its protean Waltz
as fashion barons scatter the colours of the world
on an adoring public.

I prepare the darkness
like a first kiss.

The sunlight pirouettes in beams of twisted light
dangling like limbs from our imagination,

flowering like kings
huge with crown, sunflowers
in bloom.

We enter the jungle,
tourists with awkward smiles
royalty in dungarees.

A vendetta where once a rain forest stood,
labyrinths of apology
where once a crucifix shone.
A one-night stand
with a simple trust.

Now we are these same men
we swore we would not be.
Now we can hide amongst thieves and
peasants and kings.

Now we are these same men.

Awaiting the carcinomas of old age
the platitudes of revenge.
The scorn heaped by trigger-happy politicians
on honest poets and holy men alike,
on their simple tomfoolery.

And at the gallows we will hold hands
feigning a partnership
a sympathy for old trusts.

Viva La Habana, Viva Cuba,
we charge
in a parade of bullets
and awake
crashing into the clouds.

Havana, Cuba

Grand Manan

It was the wild rabbits
that first convinced me I was human, again.
The rabbits and the tides,
reminding me old sins are immortal
and only the future can be forgotten in time.

It was first
the silence, that made of me a believer.
Then the sharp angle of water against stone
that made of me a heretic
in this most unusual of places.

But it was the unexpected rally of the flesh
the wanton caress,
that made me reconsider love.

The painful history
that brings bodies together like nations-at-war.
The lust that makes every sand beach a tourist attraction.
Each final chapter that makes of men, grown children,
and island paradises
property of the sun.

Here in the throes of good fortune
I am convinced again
that maps were made for other men
to keep me poor and forever lost in poetry.

And I observe, that we are equal
after the fact.
That fishermen make poor philosophers
but philosophers make even worse fishermen.
That there is great fidelity amongst archetypes, even
as conversations bring the continents together.

That the moon is as far away as the ocean is wide
and the cell is smaller still than either's reality.
And both bring me back to the very beginning
when reason stole my heart
before my very mind.

And where would we be

And where would we be without love,
without the sky to lie under
and pretend we are gods.
Admiring the luminous reflection
that is our one creation, our sole pursuit.
Where would we be without this day in heaven.

In churches, on review boards, in groups
of more than two clapping our hands.
Comparing poems, suffering the weather,
hanging from the day's news
in the throes of a mood.
Telling each other how to hurt
how we have suffered commonly for a cause.

The heart opens here like a small business
and we slip off our tongues.
We call it possibility, an open sky
the beginning of the end.
We become celebrities without a past
innocent, like any war criminal.

In the morning where we still lie, lovers
exhausted and wise
unlearning the alphabet
from politics, to power, to peace.
And our arms, willing students, graduate
into the next century.

Amulets

her wrists bending
the moon's hollow beams

amulets
of broken light

falling softly
on her hair

how it will all end
the crossing, the sadness.

Daisies

And where they fall
dictators and men alike
resurrect their petals
braid them into the medallions
and necklaces
they then name for the world.

And if all I have said is untrue,
it was to keep them foolishly alive
as though another poem
dapper and crowned.

The sky is bluer than usual
though it is night

angels rest on clouds.

In a Matisse painting
dadaists toss colours in the air,
light up the world.

I find them here, love
gathered in your name
its splendour
in the shape of a flower
yellow and white, under my chin
like daisies.

We have seen the movies

We have seen the movies on slavery,
the row houses and bakers fields.
The common integers of truth and beauty
and the aging juntas that have made it that way.

We have seen the small town mangers
and inimitable neon Christs.
The wise men with their sidemen pointing fingers to the stars.

My own grandparents were gassed, hidden
in sewers and farmer's attics.
Now nowhere can there be light found for their prayer.

Look there and you will see at the bend in the lake
the crane with his head hidden in the valley,
And hear the silver bells of workhorses
trudging through the snow.

So much has gone wrong in a century.
Heidegger and Wagner baiting history.
Young girls raped by puppets
of an unknowable mind,
at Mauthausen, praying for slow death to come
like an Aryan waltz.

The grass grows now over these epiphanies.
Over the cantatas and syllogisms,
the glass slippers of a century fallen.
Its skin lanterns and prayer.

Forgive me if I have not noticed you sooner.
I have loved you the only way I knew how.
Somehow it is our unfinished dreams that save us.

How we were gunrunners in the broken streets of Marrakesh.
The grand Marquis in Seville and pont Neuf in Paris
where we tossed oranges
like fallen moons.

Havana where we danced
to the Rime of the Ancient Mariner.
Reading Anna Karenina and the ballads of Varadero
in Snowdon's dark monasteries.

We know nothing of the crusaders or Spanish civil war,
the knights-errant, or dictators
who have come in our name.
The horses drawn by a tethered hand,
the whispered-lost histories of clay dragons
and confederate dolls.

The sleeves of your gown toe the rough winter air
the sonata of frozen leaves.
Your long blue scarf and fuchsia gloves
these I will remember.
The way your hair falls back
is its own story.

How you go lost
in a world of rabbits and shy flowers.
The reveries of sun and moon, ferns and wild flowers
that call your name, hidden and unnoticed there
in the brown shirts and cattails.
The denizens of green deserts and priggish stars.

I haven't the money or faith that comes with age.
My poems are frocked in a miner's dank clothing
and the small talk of waiters has done little to tame my heart.

You have always noticed simple things;
buildings where there were none
the antics of trees, scrimmage of time.
The shape of things to come.

In that small window I see your Victorian dress,
the meddling of a King and Queen.
The wading pool of imagists, the baronage
of well-taught thieves.
A dagger and a prayer.

And I imagine you gentle and kind
as a cactus sea blooms
and the day falls deftly on its back;
while elsewhere humans find their scurrilous ways
and in their lust for all things bright
commit amnesia to memory,
the sun too ancient to penetrate.

And you strangely beautiful
like a small reptile who blinks twice
before the sun is gone.

And no one drowns

You have entered my skin a thousand times
entertained my fantasy of running from the authorities
chanting Negro spirituals and my own name.

I have only now managed the magician's smile
singing from unlikely postures
arpeggios from hot tin roofs.

You have ordained it this way.
In shawls almost too holy to speak of
you began the long descent into nakedness,
prayer by prayer.
We forsook each other's courage
to lay blame on the language itself.

No longer do we preach the gospel of love
preferring instead beauty,
its unmistakable truth.
We leer from less obligatory positions,
forgive the seasons their folly.

The stage is prepared for us.
Obscured by our charity, its scaffolding,
where once we suffered bravely, howling at late-night bistros
and erroneous street corners
as now we howl at the moon and the moon alone forgives,
sets the serpent free.

And only barely did we succeed,
survive the oligarchies of the poetaster and laureate
chasing rainbows at our feet,
forgiving the rose its thorn.

Only barely.

Choosing instead the souks and cafes of old Morocco
the calamity of our own small prayer.
Casablanca where we drove for two days in the rain
for tea and a Gauloises cigarette.

This too was a mistake,
an idea before its time.

And now as you lie there
in pools of certain love
golden hair falling, calligraphy
into a gentle sea,
our journey ends
the winds subside

the gods go sailing by
and no one drowns.

We move slowly through the fire

We move slowly through the fire
vivid colours, moods of argument.

The promise is a sleeping child
and the next poem, a suit of clothes.
Our bodies are late arrivals
and the heart, a Trojan horse.

The sunset quarrels with all of this.
Laments us into place.

And we move slowly through the fire.
Past the tongue, the mouth
to the entrails.
Stubbing our toes on the darkness,
losing our hearts to the sand
wandering aimlessly through the heat.

Through fields and treatise.

Desire trumpets its arrival,
the flesh again imperial.
Beauty casts its shadow
on all the trembling faces of the day.

The night burns slowly as a candle
and love begins again.
With its fragile apology,
its clock-like arrogance
its large circumference
and vain embrace.

Love begins again
with its clairvoyant attitude
its patient eschatology,
its dilatorious star.

Here we make promises
like carnival pitchmen,
like soldiers of fortune,
with placards, with gaping wounds.
Here we are unlikely heroes
rousing the crowds.

And we move slowly through the fire
past clear sparkling stream,
blood-red sunset,
and an empty grey colossus of stone,
monuments we built
before the sky had moved.

Past wise man and priest,
the limits of their promises.
The local prophets who heralded
like moths to the fire,
compelled to heal a wound.

And we are left only with the fire.
Its swollen appetite, its cardboard tongue.
Waiting loudly to proclaim an adventure,
crestfallen.

No longer certain,
no longer able to hate, even the rich,
no sure definition, no enthusiasm
only solstice, departure.

The particular evasiveness of grace and beauty

Life is mystery.

The rose knows this
            its camisole
        raised to the shoulder
    as naked   it bends to the day.

Thorns are a reminder of its guest list.

Everything begins as planned
insects whisper their nightly versions of doom
and resurrection
        rumours dispel themselves
        colours lacerate the unending sky.

Neighbours awake to the familiar
An old tomcat wanders home

A petal
        falls

                as far away
catastrophes bloom,
everywhere
        on the horizon.

The language of Rilke

I

By night's solitary vision
must we begin,
by the lyre of a broken heart
the measure of one body against another.

In an undisclosed distance
love is blooming.
Between the petals of tulips
and chrysanthemum, a mute tongue
emerges from the dark.
Its chrysalis houses the night
renders life art.

The distance beckons us
clears a patch of light.

The day moves slowly.
The canvas finds its deepest colours.
Guests will follow.

II

In quiet parks
children masquerade
before the whore of becoming
ordinary children,
dancing the flamenco, a rose
in each mouth,
seraphim raising their arms
towards the sun. They dance
despairing of light.

The commotion arouses the trees.
They shed their leaves.
They are nude.
It is fall.

III

We awake,
to the drone of madness
medieval art,
find flowers in the hands of generals
by the bastille, a broken heart.

And love, sweet love
reappears, on the wings of dragons
on plinths of light,
the wind its chaperon,
the stars its holy night.

One more step
and we lose the language of Rilke,
our harlequin dress
our particular swan song.
We drown in a river of blood
telling ourselves
it is ordinary metaphor.

Errata

First it is the walk that changes.
Then the ability to distinguish truths.
Your neighbourhood is your own now.
You are immortal for having suffered so long.
The world is a sixth sense.

You have dreamed this by accident.
The road has been long.
You have slain giants
and are busy inventing a legend.

You hear school children in the distance.
Men and women hang evenly from the sky.
A prophet clears his throat.
There is no ideology, no politics.

Ghosts remind you that you have been betrayed
a thousand times.
A cuckold of all things.
Jung, Voltaire.
Your shadow hangs from this portrait.

There is no cross in sight.
This is part of the plan.

Paris will be there.
The gargoyles, Van Gogh.
And you. The room will be small,
thin spears of light.
Quarrels with angels.

The dumbwaiter is your only friend.
You will speak the truth.

Still you are tired
from having asked for so much.

You have waited your turn.
There is no monument for this, only night.

Your father trembles near death.
An old lover ties you to her bed.
You weigh every emotion.
Repeat your vows. Fall.

You have waited your turn.
Nothing is easily saved.

Someone has told you beauty is the face of intuition.
You have followed the shepherd here to a final calling.
You kneel for a time.

A storm is brewing. Mozart reclines.
The plowman spears the earth.

You awake, a carnival act at your feet.
You swing from the highest cloud.

Who then

After Eliot

To whom will we speak
of these things, of pity
and salvation
of ordinary human things.

And you who stood sentinel against the night.
And you who stood fast against the night.
Who now speaks to you of torture.
Who will speak for silence now.
Who will find the music left us in these final days.

(As the planets fall,
the planets fall.
Falling.
An ordinary event.)

Who now will speak for silence.

And angels and still more angels
gather in these tiny hours
of hierarchy and truth
and angels
who know poetry is pure sentience
and laughter godliness.
Angels will gather.

The words come from afar
beneath castles built of drifted sand
of sand, of dream,
of laughter itself.

Who will begin to tell the tale
when there is none,
none to tell.

And castles will sink,
one unto another
and we will be afraid,
again afraid.
Armies will disappear into the night.

Where shall we turn.
Who then must we address.

We will say salvation
mean an ordinary day,
laugh from the heart
appear silent,
unafraid, still unafraid.

We will find time for the invention of things
of beauty, of sorcery,
of invention itself.

Pity and truth
these will be ours
human things,
things that might last.

Old friends will comfort us
and later, at the table
there will be guests.

They will say
it is fine, it is good,
and we will nod,
having decided upon a different style.

And disciples will line the wall
with their chagrin,
find a garden in which to begin
the planning, the event
we might call creation.

Disciples will follow us here
at least here,
with good intent.

And we will find ourselves
only here, here at last
between all other things.
And what we know
will be ours.

Close to the ordinary we stand
for a time
keening for the sun, the warmth,
and we will say, as citizens,
there is too much to be said
to be done.
Recall love, the hard places we have been.
Say, in any case too much
and later be afraid.

We will eat, drink,
decide upon the wind
its shrillness in night
its warm breath in day.
Decide between the rich
and poor, as others have
and others must again.

The planets fall.

And we will land
and dream of other stars
where we might dream
again. Muse will appear
in the name of magic.
Malady will reign. There will be hope
despair and change, much change.

Lovers will come between mercy
and intent,
body between body.
Armies will fall.
And in the company of others
we will become others, still
be alone.

The mountains will answer us only then
in a lofty voice
with lofty intent
and the sky brawling with stars
will be storm,
and a child crying
will be only night
and a poem stillborn
between the two.

To whom will we speak of madness then.

INTERREGNUM

The flag mocks the wind for its delirium.
Each century carries its palanquin of song.

Go my poems

Go my poems, with fire by your side
and the blind eye of a falcon

with the rage of a Mercian king
and the turning manner of a great affair.

Go with a voice that gathers against itself

and with the fury of a city
that has forsaken its prophets.

Dance through the belly of the wind

by the apostate heavens
and death's own moon,

where no last truth awaits.

Of ecstasy and of green-eyed sentient beauty
sing, requiems of grey imperium.

Go where seraphim reign
and their wards would not follow,

by the barren lands of purpose and faithless interlude,
its raiment of colourless ode.

Sing the heresies of a thousand discontents
the traitorous fates,

their devilish lanterns
and broken song,

and by their silences know your way

distance upon distance
to the end of a pharaoh's line.

Unfinished Poem

Slowly the light dims
as if it were calling your name
from the apparent afar.
This might be wisdom at last
at least, or simply the light's dimming.

And you call out to find yourself
gradually ceasing,
forgotten by those whom in your love
and impatience
were patriated and lost
like some great sea,

a great extravaganza
you then must call your own.

Might you have said . . .
and been understood
a muttered prayer or chapel wandered by
a chance thought, a misgiving,

that good and bad
might have been less or more
the same,
like some ancient seafarer's dream,
Catullus before his brother's grave
meeting with the grey verities
of dawn.

And in the garrets and
great innocence of youth
before there was a prayer
to be unspoken,
there was truth
the place we have come this far to find.

Had we said love
they would have replied vaguely,
without eloquence,
insisted on surety and good measure
with all the fecundity of a pig's ear.

I would have pointed out the sun
had they not already found the moon
said it more simply
were it more simply to be said

and prayed for their deliverance
had their deliverance not been forfeited
on such emptiness as night
ceasing to be, had their own ears
not cowered by my door
my foot caught in the dark.

And in the mechanisms of small hamlets
you will find the great town hall
with its sloping patina roofs
leaning towards the wide open space
and the cool machismo of the heart.

For politics is the machinery
of will, the cooing of feathered politicians,
politicos more properly said,
pigeons contrasting brightly
with the propensity of doves.

A rare thing indeed to write
and to find in it a lover's true self
inhered in no great teaching
or learning at all
but only in the subsequence of folly
and heart of a young man
who in his way finds his deeds

and mistakes for poetry
the ordinary myth that passes for youth.

I have with these eyes seen
beauty enough to behold
a sorrow greater than love,
the last spinning of the Fall
the weather's unwavering design.

A story dramatically untold
where light narrowly meets grey,
what already has been learned
and unlearned, said and unsaid

a contentment to which place
we have come
thus far to describe

moved by sadness
and ill wind,
spring after tiresome spring
laden with farewell
its eulogy of snow,

and pity, pitiless
at last.

Hallmark

If I was a painter
it would be a pedigree colour,
blue as the face of an angered god.

The earth would take back its journey
and the night its miscellaneous tide.
The trees, and the forests among them,
the etceteras that gave birth to Eve.

A spaniel, dumb as a coot
comes jabbering my way.

The sun, too, gambols by
heals the darker verbs
that have made their way, anciently into my throat.
Stones to be unearthed.

"Nothing at all" the wind will say.
Later it too passes with the unhurrying sky.

Past the old cement works, I track time
like railroad ties.
Know my own time has come.

Play crambo with the passers by
and river's edge.
Or rhyming rhymes
with each nervy habit of enterprise,
ordering the planet to its knees.

By the old foundry
where in the hollows and crags of claw
we joined troop with the gypsy moths
and mandrakes,
waged a child's war.

Each piece of gouged stone
a parapet, from which place the apparitions fell.
Shadowless like a moat,
or gaping wound.
A finality some poets rage against.

I have walked from one room to another this way,
found myself in halls with only one light to see by.
Misted galleons and changing tides,
parishioners who invoked our trade on their behalf.

Like the Helots of Sparta
or gamekeepers of old Scottish lairds
who lived their brackish lives
enthralled upon an entrance.

And pinned to the firmament
of solitude and grey cumulous prayer
crow like intellects
and sing like drowned men.

After Keats

The young ones call me sir now
and the sapling woos another season.
And all of death, another man's bones
for whom a debonair wind has come calling.

A fine day. The nuns in dark blue
and chassidim walking with God.
By the oratoire a sea urchin sings
Nowhere do the clouds gather...

Between the tree lined boulevards
the perfect sonnets of Keats
and up above, the wind enchanted, trousers
and woollens in the fray.
A chorus line beneath which a tabby and fallen mitten
have come to terms.

I bring myself into question, obey no law,
instead steal glances at the tenured line
of dead and proven shadows,
at the Librarie in the candyshop heart of Westmount
where a gaggle of poets meet,
searching out the villanelles of a dancing bride.

The ennui of a stubborn grace
its many profiteers among them,
the velveteen hearts that come between literature
and its mad dogs.

And who was it, Shelly or Byron, who sang praises
to the novice stars
and the great soldiers who died
with the envy of battle still on their lips.

Old Lampman dreaming his imperious dream
fiercely loyal to his gentry,

the impoverished lines of Coleridge
playing the nickelodeon tunes of dawn.

The sparrows sing their hapless songs,
a tiny fractured prayer
chanting the tithes of morning.

I do not want to be where the dead reign
the cold paroxysm of night
its weeping fury,
scarps of moon and grey

and in the distance, its lioness heart
a gnarled oak
where only the sky and road meet.

Anonymity Suite

I do not think of her skirts now
nor how her parasol turns...

not even of love.

Though by her beauty impeached
still trembling

I cannot remember which of Basho's lines
I was trying to recall.

Garden Varieties

The sky has not fallen,
plinths of moon and unnamed stars
splay in her hair.
Everything is as it should be.
A wooden nickel in the hand of a fool.

I watch her stringing her prized azaleas
one half of the yard coloured in prayer.
Swarms of honeybees gather like poets
at the lilac's pursed lips.

Somehow I see Christ roaming
in the foliage of the green shade tree
hanging by the fists, teetering lovingly
from one particularly large branch,
cusps of butternut shells
and horrible
but ordinary truths, hurdling from his teeth.

And the sunlight falling.

I have stayed true to poetry
its incendiary ways,
studied and searched
for what already half the world knows.

If I have been wrong about colours
and the tiny explosion of things
let me be right at least
in the predisposition of my prayer.

For the love of her azaleas
let the finishing of a poem
be a mighty thing,
rank with grave battle
and the simplest unforgivable joy,
be like her own garden of poems
an occasion to rejoice.

I have rehearsed this death

I was busy in prayer when news came.
The night is still.
I have rehearsed this death a thousand times
forgetful now of what I most wanted to say.

Love has been good to me, more than a penitent dare,
and the small discoveries I have made
have come in between.

It is a lousy profession
barren with cut lilies and curious argyles of faith.
Gods who know nothing of the weather
and ice sculptors who masquerade in a fire-eater's robe.

Was it different in the courts of Napoleon
where sirens and shyness filled the night air.
I am wearied of this song
rehearsed this death a thousand times

followed the sun to the hybrid moon,
held to myself its secrets
the yawning traffic that follows me now everywhere
mocks my kinship and poet's despair.

It is a burden knowing how the apple blossom falls,
the say nothing and doom
of beginnings and ends we have learned ambiguously
to engage. The fallen empire,
the dunderhead of known history
and the endless chatter of priests.

And I a guildsman who fell on some luck
and learned to tell the truth.

The prayer is done. The praying is done.
There is nothing left to do.

It is not the shape of things
or their entourage, but their inevitability
that finally we must endure; the sun, its failing grace,
one last time invoked
because it is near and far.

And the moon again drags its claws
over ocean floors
cattle bones and army night,
in its womb the unspeakable beginning of time
the monk's own dance,
finally taking in its solemn way.

Parables

A mad dance, needless to say
the coffee pot knuckled down by love

shade trees dotting our graves
the language always a little farther than our dreams.

Rip van Winkle awakes at the Berlin wall
a brick on his head

scouts for morning breakfast
more hungry than wise.

Our loins are speaking in parables again,
the mud and bones of the vigil.

At the trough we recite their poor ballads
cuss and kick,

at the ordinariness of the world,
our own lives barely explained.

Of this much we are sure,
all we do is for love

and as we say it
the voice becomes our own.

Rumi's way

The burning street lamps bending like cabalist prayer.
The willowy arch of moon,
like a dromedary's imaginary shadow.

A thousand deft faces
and the ordinary occurrences of light,
the tide losing its way between god and men.

Shadows on a shadowless night.
A chalice and a bird of prey.
Two grey catapults marshalling the moon.

Poem on St. Laurent

Nothing to compare with my own suffering
searching the night out like a spinster
for the devil's own wine,
a willow's breeze chained softly to a gallows' moon.

The smell of diesel and small enough lies
vendetta and slurred speech,
crowd the parkway.
With the devil we commune, human enough
though we will die like savages.

Every word is a golden calf
tarnished silver
because we make it that way.
The long cantos of restaurateurs and cartoon versifiers
a poem in the style of our prickled youth,
the egg timer and hourglass exchanging glances.

Magic and rhythmless mind,
one yielding the other.

And you will find beauty in the hands of the betrayed,
of those whose flight has produced safety.
In the meantime you ask Homer for advice,
the legends for guidance,
and expect nothing but boulevard prayer.

Cote des Neiges, that little pharmacy
where you will find out that she is pregnant
and beg the stars with your love for her,
die a little by time.

Slay its dragon tongue,
that you may live
and she endure the leviathan,
the lilac paths
that will soon be orphaned by spring.

Eight long years and you are still beside me
though sacks of hay and forget-me-nots
litter the room.

You are already a long journey
and though we never agreed on Flaubert
or the Elizabethans
we did just now make love on the kitchen floor,
and earnestly have we argued over the Brontes and Emile
Nelligan,
the paperback riders of literature
and the necromancy of old Artaud and Verlaine,
who in great conflagration
lost the world.

And I dream my dream
blithely now,
half-awake and dying

that I by your side
have been one of them my love
though the world will stand idly by
and attest to no pardon but its own.
And only a parson's grave-side marker
might set the gavel.

You have been my friend
and I love you dearly.
I tell you this
because love is more than a promise.
The distance is yearning
and this is half the known sky.

What will be left at the long end of the day
when the parody for forgiving is lost
and all that I have
is a thousand pages of night,
struggling with the wasteland
and the mongoose of literature.

It has been a year of gradual promises
and misunderstanding.
A pastel symphony of unended colours
and fallen leaves.

All the great loves have run amok
on dry knolls,
misbegotten dreams,
their heads smitten
against the largesse of the world.

As if by chance
a sudden wind interned,
like some grey cathedral wall
standing between us
and all we have known
to be prayer.

Oratoire

It speaks to us of prayer
A gilded unearthly rhyme.
Its halls amassed
With the dead and straw voices of saints.

Stands as an auctioneer
Above the towering masses.
To the highest bidders go
The interdictions of faith.

Inside, the affairs of priests
Numbering the ascendencies,
Candles and hidden storm
Echoing silence.

But for tourists and an impediment of sky
You might imagine God
Laughing
And the angels sing its human potential.

The penitents climb its columnar towers
Stumble with the light,
The Machiavellian notions of doom.

And as a final act of parody
Carry its sail of ghostly wind
And like lemmings march gladly
Into a forbidden sea.

From the heads of scarecrows

for Chris Marks

The last minutes of the train leaving the station.
Your flaming red hair and the vestries of a fallen grace
where contrariness and stubborn night prevail.

I am glad that you have finished your poems.
The valedictories and waifs of an imagined darkness
swathed now in batches of light.

The great somnambulant moon and fields of dawn
brought down now to purpose.
Years that were not your own.

We know poetry, that great syphilitic whore
who in equal measure vandalled Catullus
and Saul of Tarsus.

The equestrians of great joy.
The sayers of great things.
The mad vicars of a sorrowful truth.

The ombudsmen who come in haste
to cure the sleeping dogs of habit,
their insomniac grappling.

And how they compete for bibelots and tea,
the omnibus of beauty
and virtuous sin.
Masters of the mere weightlessness of words.

Nothing passes here but parable and verisimilitude.
The naked truths of passersby,
Faiths and beginnings
passed about like cigars in the waiting room.

The poems left without us a long time ago.
God and women on their mind.

The suburbs rise against us
with a faith we cannot unwed
a steely unowned truth, its galvanized tongue torn
from the clubfoot morn.

It is true that we wait for nothing.
Truth is a long journey and idleness has no end.

And surely what I pass by is no less invention
than your own discursive prayer.
The faces of equanimity,
the dark traps of our imagination
that fall sadly to mystery.

I am tired old friend, as you.
Someone planted the fields to be harvested
and the sun for fallow.

Let us not exchange one set of clothes
for another.
Learn from the songs of the sparrow
the chain of command.

And let the swallows fly through broken glass,
disbelievers weave their own raven images
and Yeats speak to the albatross
from the heads of scarecrows.

Poetics

These are large issues.
Heaven and free will,
the fastidiousness of prayer.

Oh tired friend, mad with the saints
and absences of love.
No true poet believes the rumours of war.

Begin with change and illusion
then whisper the certainty of things.
Have faith in the stars, proportion
and truth.
These will not change.

Learn well the vows of a priest
and sing like a chained sky.

Absent Minded

I am tired of the way you come to me
forgiving and absent-minded about God.

For so many years you were a teacher
of unapprehendable truths.

Later those which would not rhyme
became a prisoner of some other announcement.

Do not enter the darkness
with such wistful remorse.

You are not a prophet
and your silence is not hallowed.

Wait your turn at the lobby
of eternity.

Many angels and devils have fallen precisely
where now you begin to speak.

Calliope

for Yannis

I have been reading my friend, the poets,
those ancient mariners of rhyme,
each adrift with a sun and a moon
and some grand estimate of the truth.

The Greek, Demitrius,
who tied his sail with a brood of song
and on tin backs and prayer
sailed the world.

The mad and princely ones,
who in absentia rule the penuries of night
and come to love with a terrorist's ambition
its creeds.

Italian, Dina Campany, who died in Tuscany
in the hospital for the insane,
Celine and Valladares
who wrote their gaieties in blood.
The archangel Rilke,
and Neruda who wanted to lie still with stones.

Your son smiles then,
like one of them
his eyes the portals of a blasphemous wind
a swallow's black eyes
irredeemable
like Shelley's waning moon
or the immutability of gods.

Those who sing their rhapsodies and arrogantly grieve
incline towards the light,
its bestial will
and like a moth's dizzying grace, fall.

No less angels than men.

I read the philosophers and understand little
of the ways of the world
the bastard knowledge of Democrytus
or Leibnitz's proof of God.

All of time is a dying moment
starlight and the casuistries of faith,
the chaffed sentience of men and women
who each in a different season
sing their own poor songs.

It is perhaps best a poet not judge
but stand between,
lost to the oracles of darkness where
all great faith begins.

By deathwatch and pardon
and by maddening seas.

But you Yannis why must you suffer so
for you are only six
and have already been saved from the world,
unlearned in the pantheon of sin.

Damn them all, physicians,
the gods they serve like a chalice,
the cancer that dances like a drunken reveller
about your raven soul.

How I wish you could know as I
the joy behind the failure of words,
the riven settlements of the heart
and the obeisances of beauty.

New York pedestrians quarrelling with the immensities
their newspapers holding up the rain.

Bazeball, as you say in French
now broken with a motley English pride,
your throat curdling the body's will.
Here in the greenest of mornings where still you rule.

I throw the ball
and with all the strength of Heracles
you swing, sweet child,
and its sails, oh how it sails
into a fiery sun.

Marrakesh

It is all of these damn flowers, Mohammed
lining the balconies
and gilded promenades,
that remind me of the poems of the rich.

The halcyon truths,
umbrellas and daybooks of meagre love.
Of squires and courteous nights
murmuring the prenuptials of grace.

I remember Marrakesh,
the masks of tourists and opiate moon.
The Grand Soco where the darkness stretches
like animal eyes,
and how we argued Engels
wandering the marketplace
like discovered lands.
I have returned to Paris, its twelfth *arrondissement*
the whores dancing a mazurka
on wooden tables, the smoke swirling
like a river entering the sea.

Old men sitting in anonymous cafes.
Bookstalls and lovers by the quay,
pleasure boats and the ghosts of Guillaume Apollinaire.
Everyone dressed in black.

And I remember Marrakesh
its waifs and beggars
and illegitimate tourist guides.
The harrowing weather filled with an orphan's dream.

I have seen myself the agony of the naked and dead
the broken vistas of dawn.
The ritual guilt of the housemaster
the drama of baubles and its rattle of prayer.

What has this to do with meaning,
the spectacle of hunger and deathly parade
a thousand poets long.
The highwayman's shameful philanthropy
and the libretto of the executioner's song.

Artists grappling with each new truth
taking shape beneath a Shakespearean sky
its long circumference of night,
one twilight outlasting another.

Distances

A storm gathering is easily seen
Not so blindness and prayer.

Death is also mysterious.
Like migratory birds
Who carry with them our silences
Like stone.

Untitled

For love is only this,
a season of fallen leaves
codas of silence.

In love we may hide
pray, dance,
measure the distance between skies.

Entertain dragons as priests,
and of the ordinary make
fallow for stars.

In love too, we may
arrange the order of things
forfeit the past.

The muse is of many names.
Music one. Fire another.
Magic too.

Love finally is cause
descends upon us like sky,
revelation.
Finds us thus,
naked
and yearning.

Narrowly catching light
under the mistletoe,
the barren oak betrayed.

Angels tittering
over each unfinished poem.
The devil glare-eyed and sad
at so many being saved.

Interregnum

Your picture of the Mexican hangs on the wall.
A talisman of unerring youth.

I came to you early
to announce the death of kings
and garden flowers,
to warn you against preparing a voice
to answer another's calling.

In a field far away dusk gathers
penance,
as we prepare for the event
we cannot name.

In the Negev you tamed the desert,
the dromedaries and the Mediterranean behind you.
You were there as a light post
far inland from the sea
its conch of unsung masts and heroes.

The suburbs spoke to me then
of the silence of crowns.
I was on the side of miracles
and a lover's disobedience.

The seasons change.

Many roads wind to bitter disrepute
untangle in a prophet's hair.

I knew early their treason,
the motives of grief,
before they found me wanting.

You passed on to me Rumi,
a menagerie of stone.
Your voice spoke of an earthly plan.

A butcher or seer, you said,
both endear the favour of the pretended gods.
Leave before the intercourse begins
and bring no memory home.

I held on to the wind
with the urgency of a simple trade.
The way seraphs and poets are damned
for being so close to god.

It has gathered in me, like a speed,
a journey that has nowhere left to go.
For I too have prayed and sanctified the enemy
and now must wear his clothes.

If it must end let the word pass on
as though it had never been given,
like the water drawn from the scorched hands
of a fearless desert tribe.

Let us leave untitled all that has come between us
for it is already consecrated ground.
The flag mocks the wind for its delirium,
each century carries its palanquin of song.

Logos

for Dag

You were a young emigre
from the East,
a shepherd who had left his father's house.
My father, a Polish Jew,
who too had been dispossessed
held out his hand, as you do now.

What is the weather
that it decides our fates,
comes between strangers
and the lives we obey.

I have been a criminal and a lady's man.
Neither has benefited my soul.
The rivers that will outlast our names
run dry,
like men who suffer ambition and creed.

The young want pyrotechnics and Rome.
The old find in their beginnings mercy.
You ask the simplest of things
that a man be honest and kind
and the earth be proof of his will.

Revolution and the practicums of knowledge
will not change,
nor the laws governed by nature
or as you say "the good yes and the good no".

The afflictions of the poor go on
like the valleys and mountains they must climb.
(for truth can be spoken
over and over and still remain only the truth)

Who will say that a simple grace
is not mightier
than the Baal Shem Tov
or the mysteries of Kabbalah.

On your land you dream of wisdom,
changelessness and truth.
Through the lashing winds and darkness
always in the direction of hope.

The wild geese laugh above us,
lament our human intentions.
In your heart the gods speak mutedly
of their imperfect deeds.

I hear their prayer.

Terminus

The river breaks its journey
of frozen wind and pantomime.
Sheds its wax skin
and slatternly prayer.

The weather near-sighted
and paranoid
imagines itself a fallen thing.
Moth-eaten like last year's parasol.

Newts and turtles
awaken from their slumbered rhyme.
Like mandarins arise
to the rumours of war.

And the pigeons like philosophers
stand aggrieved
on tin roofs and porticoes.
Lean against the unspokeness.

As the poor inherit the world,
the grey and blue skies
that pass us by
each like a lover's dream.

• Cap-Saint-Ignace
• Sainte-Marie (Beauce)
Québec, Canada
1996